How Will the Heart Endure?

Poems by

Alan Catlin

Cover image by Gene McCormick
Author photo by Valerie Catlin
Cover design by Shay Culligan

ISBN: 978-1-63980-387-3

Kelsay Books
502 South 1040 East, A-119
American Fork, Utah 84003
Kelsaybooks.com

How Will the Heart Endure?

For Ted Jonathan. i.m.

“If you photographed the real
Diane Arbus, who would we see?
A cranky, crying girl,
always hot and tired.”

—Maggie Jaffe, “Photos by Diane Arbus”

Acknowledgments

Café Review: "A Super Star at Home," "Andy Warhol's Three Sisters"
Ekphrastic Review: "Asked to explain," "Diane Arbus held," "Selected images from the collage wall," "Avedon, and the Collage Wall," "Eva Rubenstein's Diane Arbus Seated Before the Collage Wall," "Untitled #1–#10"
Muddy River Review: "Arbus Triplets in Bed"
Nixes Mate: "Mother Cabrini: a disinterred saint . . ."
One Trick Pony: "Diane Arbus on the Waterfront"
Parting Gifts: "Lisette Model's Feet," "The Vertical Journey," "After the Closing of the Dime Museum"
Pine Hills Review: "My Dream Date with Diane Arbus"
Rensselaerville Poem a Day Project: "Untitled #10"
Sheila Na Gig: "Untitled #2"
Turtle Island: "Small-Town Women, circa 1913"

Brief, occasional passages may have been paraphrased from firsthand accounts.

Contents

1. Arbused

How Will the Heart Endure?

Diane Arbus was an
"Emergency in Slow Motion,"

was, maybe, not planning
to die when she killed herself

as one psychobiographer suggested

She may have
wanted her functioning body

to cease

but the work to go on

which still sounds like suicide to me

especially when you slice tendons as you slit your wrists
And overdose of barbiturates

No faint-hearted attempt that

When her married-to-another lover found Diane
she wasn't just dead in her bathtub

she was dissolving

"It is hard to say what you can
put into poetry. It has to be something
you've lived."

—Robert Lowell

If a photograph is an image
then a poem can be the sum
of images that a poet uses
words to create.

Are they equal, in any sense,
to the word?

Do you have to have lived
in hell to describe it?

Diane Arbus said of taking pictures
at a nudist colony,

"It's a little bit like walking into
a hallucination without being sure whose it is."

Are the image and the poem
two parallel lines that meet in
another dimension?

One that is so remote the most
familiar objects seem incongruous
in their reality

Threatening even

One might ask:

The photographs she left behind
are all self-portraits
in hell and places nearby

Which one are you in?

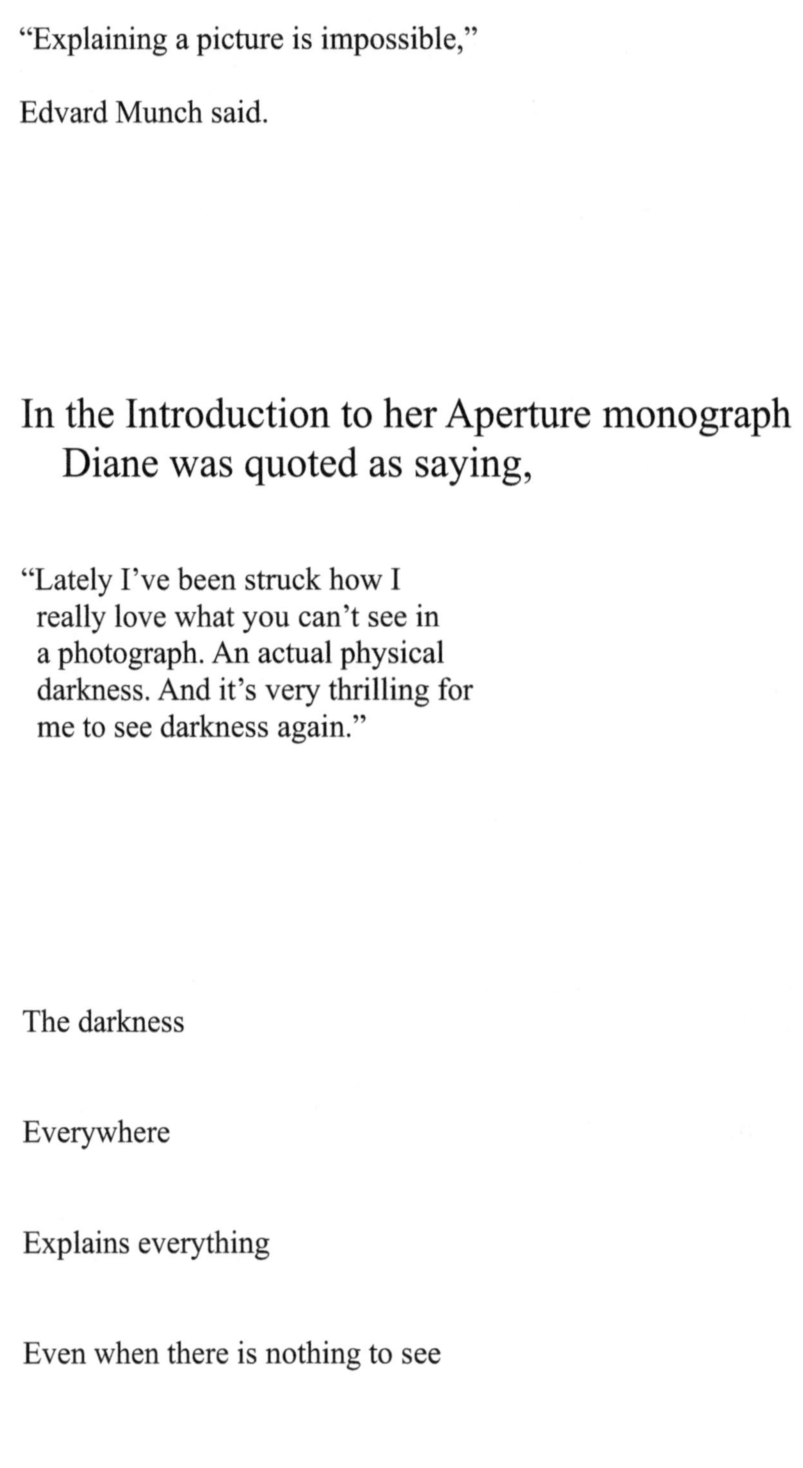

“Explaining a picture is impossible,”

Edvard Munch said.

In the Introduction to her Aperture monograph
Diane was quoted as saying,

“Lately I’ve been struck how I
really love what you can’t see in
a photograph. An actual physical
darkness. And it’s very thrilling for
me to see darkness again.”

The darkness

Everywhere

Explains everything

Even when there is nothing to see

Alan Sillitoe said,

“Well, it’s a good life and
  a good world, all said and done
  if you don’t weaken.”

Arbus negatives

I think of all those contact sheets
in the dark room of her heart

all those souls on fire

Those eyes
those facial expressions
the body languages

revealing everything
repressed

what was
previously trapped
inside

I think
what the Native Americans said
about a photograph stealing your soul
is true

It’s a silent killer

How it leaves nothing behind

Diane Arbus Meets John Berger

"Work well. We have little else.
  Trust your imagination a little more."
                                        —John Berger

Her photos are a confession

But

of what,
I wonder
      ?

"Toward dusk last night
I thought I saw the dim form
of the one I love—
now brought to me again
by haze around the dawn moon."
—Shotatgu

Early biographical essays about Diane
speculated about the nature of the sexual
experimentation she shared with her older
brother, the award-winning poet,
Howard Nemerov. They wondered
just how far they went.

They suspected but . . . .

The latest biographer, Arthur Lebow
says,

unequivocally,

they fucked

Never stopped fucking

The last time when Howard saw her
just before for she died

they fucked

What would the gutter presses have said if THEY knew:
?

SUICIDIAL ARTIST FUCKS BROTHER AND THEN SHE SLITS HER WRISTS

With a lede like that, who needs an article?

If there were any poetic justice

in this life Diane's favorite book would have been:

Secret Sharer

But there is no evidence of this

There is no evidence of poetic justice in this life
either

The subjects may have been strangers when they meet

but Diane was intimate with
all her people

Seduced them with her camera
and her voice

And they submitted,
gave into her:

their need to be seen,
really seen by someone else

an urge greater
than the urge for self-protection

Many of them felt betrayed
when they saw the results

With good reason

One even spit on her photo at an exhibition

Still,

there was no denying the fierceness of her need
the will to possess
yes, she seduced them all

even the freaks

Especially the freaks

Near the end she slept with all the subjects

anyone who asked

indiscriminately

"It's hard to tell where
you leave off and the camera
begins."
—Susan Sontag

Sontag hated Diane's work:

Said it was degenerate

and lacking in humanity

I think it was Diane's teacher
Lisette Model who said of
Sontag,

"She knows everything but
understands nothing."

Model, a well-known teacher
and ace photographer

in her own right, is best known

for the ultimate anti-fashion photo

of a morbidly obese woman posing at the edge

of the ocean on a Coney Island beach

The psychotherapist, Schultz insists

Model denounced Diane's work posthumously

after saying she had been her best student

called her work pathological

indicative of a declining mental state

this may be so

Still, Lisette gave Diane

permission

to pursue her signature

subjects: freaks

Now she is mostly known as

the teacher of Diane Arbus

“But there’s a kind of power thing
about a camera. I mean everyone knows
you’re carrying some slight magic
which does something to them.
It fixes them in a way.”
—Diane Arbus

Lisette Model’s Feet

In the darkroom, taking shape
from negative light, thousands
of pairs of bare feet, some
reclining, bottom sides out,
unclad for beach fronts, wrinkles
describing lifelines, spent pleasures,
glorious defects, others tagged at
the right big toe, named or
unknown, still others captured
from above, taken waist high,
bones revealed close to the flesh,
veined and gnarled by misuse,
carbuncular, scarred, tattooed
Yin and Yang on opposite sides,
some cut by surgeries, others
not at all, mates to the millions
of unmatched shoes left by
soon to be dead men and women,
walking along the main highway,
just before the fall of Saigon.

Model's work is animated, imbued
with life as if it were a frozen moment in time.

According to Model, Diane's photos are possessed

"Magic, that's what it's all about.
It's finding the magic. That's all
I try to do is find the magic."
—Jean Michael Basquiat

The Vertical Journey:
Six Movements Within the Heart of the City

"me and that old woman sorrow . . ."
In bum-fucked night, down Bowery
bottlenecks, under Coney Island
boardwalks, nighttown rings lower
than hell, sideshows, and freak-out's,
money lenders extending the temples
of greed, group groping the far edges
of sex, everything saleable has a price,
even the freaks: Tattoo Jack, the masked
man, out staring everyone, even Death;
Uncle Sam of the deadbeat alleyways,
flag suits and top hats he hides his product in,
no one too young or too innocent to be recruited,
dope is dope and money is money, one comes
with the other, who cares who buys as long
as the cash is green; Willie Mack, sage of
the wilderness, house of the risen sun pad
under an EL, all the way downtown,
rat-hole cellar dump filled floor to ceiling with
two-dollar ninety-eight cent jugs, labels that
read PARADISE, something offered, never received,
nearby baby carriages for the dead soldiers, the headless dolls,
all the junk that fits,
coffee cans filled with butts, lost keys,
dead insects, roaches, "anything once living
can be food," so sayeth Madam Sandra,
the ancient hausfrau, everyone's suburban
grandmother with her all-seeing black ball,
three-dollar sessions reveal all but what people
most want to know how and when; white cellar
rooms in Bellevue, clean sheets for the deceased,
toe tags for an unknown man, hanging loose for all to see.

Diane learned everything she needed to know

about portrait taking from August Sander

simply by looking:

Painter's Wife, circa 1926

after August Sander

Grosz might have used her
as a life study for his degenerate
Art.

Was someone Isherwood
would have met and been at home with
in Berlin between the two
world wars.

Was the kind who danced
too close with other women
while dressed in men's clothes
and who knew all the words to
"Falling in Love Again," a song
she felt as only a woman could.

She might marry but she would
never have children.

Small-Town Women, circa 1913

after August Sander

Were the troops marching then?
All those Kaiser boys with pointed
helmets . . .
Yes, maybe, no . . .

If they weren't, they would be
soon enough.

And these would be the women
they left behind: the somnolent, after-tea sit ins
almost relics, time frozen
as eternal girls that got left behind.

One young woman emanating a kind of,
let's-have-sex-as-soon-as-we-can- appeal
to the camera and to what waits beyond.

The other, more modest,
the large black bow at her neck
suggestive of mourning clothes
they will soon be obliged to wear.

". . . Photographs can be enigmatic. They sometimes work because of what is included in the frame, and sometimes because of what is not. There is no formula for taking pictures. It's a mysterious process; an endless challenge. Ideas for projects are constantly unfolding and possibilities reveal themselves around every corner. The trick is to be open enough to recognize them the moment they appear and driven enough to pursue them."

—Mary Ellen Mark, *American Odyssey*

After the Closing of the Dime Museum & Flea Circus

"If you've ever talked to somebody
with two heads you know they know
something you don't."
—Diane Arbus

Underwater lights in over-chlorinated
indoor pool gives off a toxic light,
gray green and shimmering, surreal as
the party goers sipping drinks from
plastic cups: high balls and fruit punches
with tiny umbrellas, mimosas colored red
as a Hawaiian Sunset, long neck beers,
some with straws for better access,
drinking all the way down to the end.
Function sign outside the pool room,
the thick-with-condensation sliding glass
double doors, says "Welcome Freaks,"
they who are gathered here one last time
after closing of last Flea Circus on the circuit;
all those sideshow attractions: bearded ladies,
one-trick-pony dwarf albinos, sword swallowers
and fire eaters, armless twins, deformants all,
medical curiosities and their touts, all unwanted
and unemployed, dressed in their costumes;
their glitter and their glow in the harsh, damaged light.

Separation and Divorce of Diane and Allan Arbus

Is it possible

Diane only loved one man

despite her willful promiscuity?

Fell in love with Allan when she was thirteen

and married him as soon as she was legally adult

Despite separations and subsequent divorce,

they remained close

Were soulmates

and had sex, no doubt, as the spirit moved and

opportunity allowed

Diane took their two girls when they broke up

Allan paid support

Would send money whenever he could

as long as she was alive

For years they shared a darkroom

“My new girlfriend now describes
our bedroom as a ‘cathedral
of erotic misery.’”
—David J Thompson

Asked to explain

the prevalence of
nudity in her
photographic work,
Diane Arbus appeared
on stage at a University
of Florida naked, like
some kind of wigged out
rock star, authorities
must have thought, as
they escorted her from
the dais, though nothing
could have been further
from the truth.
More important to Diane
was she was paid,
as she hated giving lectures,
teaching, and all that personal
appearance stuff, only taking
those assignments when
desperate for rent, food,
a new camera and, sometimes,
clothes.

“Don’t think about making out,
just get it done. Let everyone else
decide whether it’s good or bad,
whether they love it or hate it.
While they’re dealing make even
more art.”

—Diane Arbus

Diane Arbus on the Waterfront

Still life on the Coney Island boardwalk,
beach people stunned by the sun, struck
senseless, burned beneath their paisley
flowered robes and ruined straw hats.
Their eyes framed by rhinestone rimmed glasses,
noses tipped by an oily white substance, fat fingers
curling about the cones of the cotton candies.
In the background, over the shoulders
of these thieves of time carrying away their
brief imitations of immortality in embroidered,
woven bags, are the booths for amusements,
games of chance vaguely out of focus
but with just enough clarity, you can almost
hear the voices of the barkers calling out,
you can almost see the photographer rewinding
the film, deliberately double exposing,
a superimposition of carnival freaks
and the lemming people from the beach,
on the last roll she ever shoots.

“When people look at pictures, I want them to feel
the same way they do when they read a line of a poem twice.”
—Robert Frank

Diane Arbus held

a print of her
photograph
of a boy caught
in a candid
moment: geeky
smile, skinny
arms and legs,
bony knees,
suspender straps
sliding down his
no-muscle-arms,
short pants soon
to follow, and
a hand grenade
in his left
hand, an almost
incidental detail
that warm, bright,
summer day in
Central Park 1960
whatever, she said,
“For me the subject
of the picture is always more
important than the picture.
And more complicated.”
Words spoken a few
months before her suicide.

"Your poetry issues of its own accord when you and the object have become one—when you have plunged deep enough into the object to see something like a hidden glimmering there. However well phrased your poetry may be, if your feeling is not natural—if the object and yourself are separate—then your poetry is not true poetry but merely your subjective counterfeit."

—Basho

"Well, I shall ask forgiveness
for having lived on lies."
—Rimbaud

Could you imagine Ozzie and Harriet,
America's quintessential, middle class,
no-conflict couple in bed?

Diane could

She did David and Ricky too with their families,

not necessarily in bed

Happy, Happy, Happy Nelsons
according to Esquire photo caption

We all know what happened to Ricky, don't we?

Ricky of that fatal rendition of "Free Bird"

Just another "American Pie" day the music died
rock star

"She (Diane) was very sexy. She told stories about each of her photographs, and she had a great sexual anecdote for every picture, and by the time she was finished we were all in love with her.

"You just felt like you could tell her whatever your sexual fantasy was and she would understand—there was no taboos. She was very wound up about photography. She talked fast, breathlessly as if there was not enough time to get it all out."

So said Stephen Frank, photographer,
about being in a class taught by Diane

My Dream Date with Diane Arbus

The place of our meeting decided well
in advance, after dark, in a theater on
forty second street. The feature we will see,
"Freaks." I am the man too large for the room
I am confined in, and she, the lady in the wheelchair
wearing the fairy princess Halloween mask,
a pinwheel braided into her fright wig,
a magic flute hanging from a leather
strap around her neck she will blow
as I wheel her through the stalls,
down the long sloping aisles, entreating
the triplets and the twins to throw their sweets
into the wide-open trick or treat bag held
on her lap. The movie is not the black and white
"Freaks," set in a traveling carnival, starring midgets and dwarves,
pinheads, and hydros,
but the one where all the actors are people
from real life, wearing paper faces cut from pages of the daily
news, all of them frozen in stilled lives,
enacting crimes of the century: imperialist wars
of occupation, assassinations, and atrocities,
ritual torture and extreme rendition,
the starkest of them all, a boy in short pants
holding a hand grenade, pin pulled, his face
contorted, anticipating what happens after
the momentary pain.

Eddie Carmel was the name of the man

known in Arbus' world as the Jewish Giant

Was eight foot nine inches tall

He wanted to be known as the World's Largest
Comedian

Spent most of his adult life as a side show
attractions with names like The World of Mirth

He didn't get to do many Stand-up routines

Mostly he just stood up

As young as the age of 15, Eddie recognized
he was not normal. Said to himself, "I am
a freak."

Still, whenever someone called him a "freak"
to his face, he cried

Eddie had occasional work in the movies

One of his roles was in the classic cult
flick, "The Brain That Wouldn't Die."

It was such a bad movie you could easily
imagine the Mystery Science Theater crew
critiquing, the flimsy, ridiculous plot,
the horrendous acting, the pitiful props . . .

All of it, just this side of ten-dollar budget,
Ed Wood movie

Ironically, before he died, Eddie had a rare
condition that caused him to shrink six
inches

The Jewish Giant from "The Brain That
Wouldn't Die" became "The Incredible
Shrinking Man."

“When Donne wrote *no man is an island*
Godzilla wasn’t real yet, slept in the Pacific
until the bomb shook its little-boy fist
and he wandered into the studio.”
—Sadiko Murakami

Diane said, “You know how every woman has nightmares when she’s pregnant that her baby will be born a monster? I think I got the mother’s face as she glares up at Eddie, thinking, ‘Oh my God, no!’”

What did Diane dream when she was pregnant?

Diane pregnant

dreams of white
washed gallery
walls, long, narrow
corridors sloping
downward into the dark.
On the walls
are all the framed
pictures of every
crying baby
she ever shot.
All of them
silently weeping,
crying way beyond basic
needs, so insistent
in their weeping,
the museum glass
dissolves,
the frames melt,
as well, until
there are just
shrunken heads pinned
to temporary walls,
heads a sickly
pink, like baby
doll heads severed
from their bodies.
She is no long
looking, no longer
observing, but
looking away,
trying to escape
the inescapable,
the walls pressing
tight against her
but she can
no longer cry out

This is the dream I imagined
Diane might have had

I expect hers were much, much worse

2. Group Portrait with Freaks

“Try & watch a horror film
from the point of view
of the monster.”
—Sam Sax, “It’s Alive”

“We keep our eyes open, but
we no longer think.”
—Faludy, “Realism and Empiricism”

Selected images from the collage wall in Diane Arbus's last apartment

Gruesome newspaper headlines
burning car pictures
like Warhol
silk screens

it's not the color
but the absence of it

it's all about
the bodies

and the blood

Front page murder stories
victims lying
in blood puddles
stained "body bag"
sheets

Torn, rough prints,
of Vineland home
for Down's Syndrome
adults

An American patriot
face

gone, man,
on America

love it or leave it,
with flag pennant

A Bellocq naked whore,

The ones with a scratched
out faces, presumably,
unabashed, nude whores

The girl with glittering
lipstick

The World's Fattest Woman

Group Portrait of
Hubert's Dime Museum
freaks

Unearthed, ancient
desiccated skin,
and skeletal remains

Autopsy stills
halfway through
the procedure

The soiled and
the impure

Pictures at an Exhibition

Her life

Diane Arbus Spellbound

She feels as if
her life had become
a nightmare sequence
of Dali dreams

As if she were sliding
downhill on an icy slope
through a clock
with no hands

As if she had woken up
on a spiral staircase
in ascent

Walking up a Mission
bell tower despite
a mortal fear of heights

Now more afraid of
climbing than the destination

Feels unable to stop,
compelled upwards, even
when a falling body is seen

Is unsure of where she is
where the body came from,
where she is going
where she will end up

On the top
or at the bottom

As if trapped in
an Escher landscape
with dead things in it

Does not know which
body is hers:

The fallen one or
the one already disposed of

Does not know where she will land
or if she will land at all

Jumping appears to be
an option, but what if
she floated, and rose, instead
of plummeted and fell?

Where would she end up then?

There does not appear
to be a solution to this
dilemma

Waking up is not an option

Avedon and the Collage Wall

Avedon thought Diane's new
Westbeth apartment was more
airy

had more ambient light
more life

than the previous one
that felt more like a lair,
a cave, than an actual living space

except for the collage wall

except for all those murder book
displays:

tattered rough contact sheet freaks,
and cutting room floor

portraits, missing all but
their toe tags

even had a toe tag
morgue shot

he almost missed on
this Naked City,
real life,
splatter porn wall

The wall of
dead bodies,
human rejects
Weegee wannabee,
bad guys and mob hits,

all those crazy
deranged,
dead
and Down’s people . . .

Living with that
had to affect your
mind

he thought

A year later
she was dead

After Diane died Avedon said
to a former assistant,

"I would give anything to
have her talent."

The former assistant said,
"No, you wouldn't."

Eva Rubenstein's Diane Arbus Seated Before the Collage Wall

Diane looks older than she is
or ever would be

A woman in leather pants
and a dark shirt

Only a couple of years removed
from being mistaken for the sister
of her oldest daughter

Before the hepatitis
she naively asked a friend about,

"Can you get hepatitis from anonymous
sex?"

Before the orgies she filmed and
took part in

The persistent money woes
Married lover troubles

The depression
that fueled her fear
of losing her looks

She appears as a person
who no longer cares what
she eats if she eats

Who thinks,
“What would be the point
of eating?”

Of anything

Sitting, as she is before
the collection of death, destruction,
doom

Not long before she would
become, “Portrait of the artist
three days dead in her bathtub”

Mary Ellen Mark, Edward Simmons, South Bronx, H.E.L.P. Shelter, NY, 1993 an *American Odyssey* photo

Whose idea, was it?
To dress that black child in a medieval
headsman's dark hood at H.E.L.P.
in the Bronx?
A costume for trick or treating, sure,
but a kind of sick joke, as well?
Giving the kid a plastic axe for
severing heads from bodies.
Fake movie blood,
Maybe even a wax head in a bag
to carry with you on the candy runs
And where would those runs be?
In a neighborhood where severed
heads may be a fact of life?
Maybe more real than a child could ever
know?

This innocent one in shabby shelter
room, orphaned or abused?
abandoned or disowned?
Living the last fantasy of a childhood
interrupted and on the verge of
an adult life where Help and Hope
were places where he once lived.

See his eyes.
How dilated they are.
Excited doesn't cover it.
It's almost as if he could see the future.
That he knows: after the axe falls
there is no way to change
what happens next.

“It was my teacher, Lisette Model,
who finally made it clear to me that
the more specific you are, the more
general it’ll be.”
—Diane Arbus

I told an artist friend I was doing
an Arbus project.

He said,” Why don’t you just kill
yourself and save a whole lot of
pain and suffering?”

He said the same thing when I
told him I was doing a Bergman
retrospective.

I’m still here.

He’s not.

Diane’s long distance, nighttime,
Walk for Peace shot, atypical for
the angle, the framing, the perspective.

Suggests the peasant’s and the knight’s
Dance to the Music of Time with Death
in the Final Scene of “The Seventh Seal.”

Love and Death.

Inadvertent double exposure for a self-portrait and images of Time Square NYC, 1957

This is how life scrolls by when
images are twinned, when everything
is double exposed by design or otherwise.

Everything is random, chaotic,
images like a home movie, viewed backwards
your life devolving into something negative
a black hole of memory nothing
escapes from

Here a blonde Janet Leigh look alike,
circa 1960, screen testing for
a shower scene in a Hitchcock movie,
once seen, is impossible to forget

Striding purposefully, NYC style,
a lit cigarette in her right hand

Bright light marquees/
adverts, blurs of available light,
slipping off the edges of an image,
into the night

over the heads of two men walking

Of two old ladies talking in
their night-on-the-town ensembles,
low heel sensible shoes,
black overcoats that may never have
been in style

The one-way side street off Times Square
sign pointing crosstown

over the heads of a gesticulating man
raving to a crowd, of unseen-by-everyone
but-him, listeners

An unfurled American flag held by an
unseen hand at the made mute by time's
exposing lens, man

Then back on the Square in neon blare
and blur

A vertical sign, floors high that says:
MANHATTAN

and the grim face super-imposed on
this panoramic series of shots:

the artist is watching
with wide eyes

is looking inside you

revelations

"They are the proof that something was there
and no longer is. Like a stain. And the stillness
of them is boggling. You can turn away but when
you come back they'll still be there looking at you."
—Diane Arbus in a letter on her work
to the Fogg Museum 1971

"O faithless and perverse generation
how long shall I be with you?"
Matthew 17:17

Nemerov, he dead

Diane photographs her father
on his death bed

in hospital

shrunken by cancer

Shoots an old lady
mouth open in a white
room in white light,

more dead than alive
if, in fact, she is alive

in a white room, where
the color of death is the absence
of all things living,

all the colors life offers

Shoots an autopsy in progress,
toe tag still hanging
on the body in parts,

in another white room
in another room
inside the same place
as the others

Death is not her best subject

"Dead artists are easier to deal with."
—Lubow

A number of years ago, I was with some poets, visiting Bernadette Mayer in her home, in her self-proclaimed, Poetry Forest. She was trying to decide what poems to read for a program honoring her at the State University of New York, Buffalo. Was unsure whether to read new work or older stuff, more familiar work or, maybe, something to shake them up a little. Implying: nothing much written, especially poetry, shakes people up anymore. Unable to decide she says, "I think they prefer their honored poets to be dead."

Implying, I assumed, as it always was, it still is.

And now she is dead too.

"My name is exile. My name is anguish.
My name is longing."

—Angela Carter

Spontaneous Siamese Twins

after Diane Arbus

They are the carnival clowns,
lost thrill seekers, dressed for being
dragged down a strip of life; she wearing
pedal pushers four sizes too small,
clipped together at the waist, blue butterfly
tattoos rising above each stretch lined hip,
set free to seek sagging braless breasts,
her love bitten, uncovered neck, bruised,
bloodlines ascending into a tangle of unwashed
hair, she smiles for the camera, for her lover boy,
exposing a mouth of missing teeth,
fever sores, lesions.
Linked arm and arm, she walks with her man,
punch drunk and crazy, he wearing his sleeveless
denim jacket, his smiling death head stained
by wash and wear motor oils, homemade black
tattoos proclaim: Too Bad To Live,
Let It All Hang Out, Let It Bleed;
their backs hunched forward they make their
way into the night, time junkies in search of a hit.

Still Death

Watching short film about creation
that embraces death

I think of the black and white photo titled, Still Death: a bowl
of fruit rotting

And then I think of her self-portrait that could have been titled:

Still Death in a Bathtub Posed like Marat
as Performed by Diane Arbus

But this is not a poem
about Watching Television/
Amusing Yourself to Death

or about being killed on TV

Nor is it about what God Wants
God Gets but an Infinite Jest,

one that references Jim Morrison who said:

"Petition the Lord with Prayer—
I will not petition the Lord with Prayer."

Maybe he should have
petitioned the Lord with poems

He might have lived longer

She might have as well

Hubert's Dime Museum

Last of its kind in
the Naked City

freak shows and weird
revues

nestled among ten cinemas
each showing
a different kind of
double,
even triple feature:

Westerns, gangster flicks, comedy . . .

All just a terrorist bomb's toss
from Times Square

Hubert's,
where Arbus found
subjects for her
signature,

her breakthrough work:

The Vertical Journey,
The Full Circle . . .

Where the Jewish Giant
was billed as: The World's
Largest Cowboy

Where Jack Dracula
displayed 300-odd
tattoos

Where Tiny Tim played as Larry Love

had short hair
and didn't wear a suit

I'd have paid extra
to have seen that

I guess people did

Pay that is

Before Hubert's closed down
and the cinemas became
stroke houses
and shooting galleries

Where, once, the Midnight
Cowboy strolled by
a few tricks short
of a pay day

> "A photograph is a secret about a secret. The more it tells you the less you know."
> —Diane Arbus, Artforum 1971

> "Nothing is ever the same as they said
> it was. It's what I've never seen before
> I recognize."
> —Diane Arbus, Artforum 1971

In her last years, Diane recounted dreams to her therapist.

Dream Sequences

Dreamt of the doctor who was a giant
who didn't listen to anything she had to say

And never responded

Split, instead, into dozens of little men
who scurried in different directions

There was no way of knowing which one
to pursue

She felt that,

"You are dead when you ask
  the doctor why you are sick
  and he doesn't hear you."

Diane dreams of being on
a sinking ocean liner
gleefully taking pictures

Diane dreams of being in a burning
house. Though she is surrounded
by flames, she is not personally affected
by the conflagration
Nothing stops her from taking pictures

Except herself

Those rolls of film
Would they ever have been developed?

What would those pictures have looked like?

I Pose a Question:

There was a Psychiatric Center on Long Island
not far from where Diane was living.

At the peak of her creative life was
also, the peak time for mental health
admission/ incarcerations

Thousands of waiting-for-someone like her
shock treatment patients
schizoids
depressives
catatonics
even some violent offenders

Eisenstaedt shot there
extensively before the War

At one point you could even
take a train there

Why didn't Diane shoot there?
She shot everywhere else

Do you think,
maybe it was too close
to home?

A Super Star at Home, 1969
According to Diane Arbus

Diane lied to Viva

she lied to all her unclothed
subjects

saying she would only shoot
their faces

That nothing would show

She always revealed everything

Naked from the waist up,
Viva looks as if she is nodding,
deeply drugged,
maybe just this side of overdosed,

or dying,

eyes rolled all the way up into her head
under half-closed lids

When she stands
from where she is lying
during the shoot,

this late portrait
could have been
retitled:

Revenant Rising

Arbus's Triplets on a Bed

These hesitant identical
adolescents
unsure of themselves

in their private space
bedroom

so close together
they are almost
conjoined

seeking safety in
numbers

defense from this
adult lady with a
camera sweet talking

coaxing them out of comfort
zones toward another
place

and indefinable place
only the camera can see

They will never
be this close
again

Andy Warhol's Three Sisters

Not the weird ones
like Macbeth's three witches
but the McGuire ones

No one was more famous
than they were

once upon a time
though now barely a memory

perfect Warhol subjects
as only he could know
fame's transitory nature

All of them dressed
in formal black with full veils

Maybe at a funeral?
But who smiles at funeral?

Or are the identical smiles
just reflexive on their part
whenever a camera is near?

Or are they
the ultimate Pop Art Polaroids

Maybe on the way to
one of Capote's infamous
black and white parties

celebrating his latest face lift

fresh wounds showing,
stitches as well

“I always thought I’d like my own tombstone
to be black. No epitaph, and no name—

“Well, actually, I’d like it to say, ‘figment.”

Said Andy Warhol in *America*

Group Portrait with Freaks

Composed as they are, these
almost innocents, in daylight,
become something sinister after
dark. Their gathering here,
on back steps of traveling circus
caravan, is not for a portrait but
for a council of war. All these
misshapen human oddities,
destined to sideshow tents, ten cents
for extra displays:

hunchback dwarfs,
human rubber band man,
female Siamese twin sisters,
half man-half woman,
triplet pinhead women
subhuman all, to the "Normals."
Normals who are contemptuous of
the fraternal creed of freaks:
"An attack on one of us is an attack
on all of us."

Once the plan is final, once the rain
has begun, night has fallen, the offenders
against the creed, a strongman and
a trapeze artist, will cease their superior
being act, and become prey, hunted by
this strange crew, bearing knives to
exact their revenge. Those knives that
seemed so harmless in daylight, become
instruments of torture, implements of
surgeries unseen, surgeries that make
the strongman, the fatman of the future,
the beauty, the beast. The show is traveling
still. A quarter buys a picture suitable for
framing, for hanging on a wall.

“Yet darkness honestly lived through
is a place of wonder and life. So much
has come from this.”

—Robert Lowell

3. Portfolio: Untitled and Otherwise

Diane's Lists of potential subjects and general topics:

morgue freak at home; jewel box revue; roller derby women;
dressing rm; woman's prison; weird women; paddy wagon;
meat slaughterhouse; tattoo parlor; taxi dance hall-before hrs.;
lonely hearts club; Happiness Exch.; lady wrestling;
beggars-blind; place waterf., hotel;
ladies room-coney-subway; daughters of J dying.

subjects

crime; despair, sin; madness; death; fame; wealth; innocence.

A Grace for the Meal Coming

"Thanks to the sun, the earth, and the earthworm,
thanks to the worker in the field and hearts
through whom this food comes to the table, we
receive, as for the dead, these preparations."
—Cid Corman

House of Horrors Coney Island

In daylight, this place seems like
just another rundown roadside
attraction:

worn, iron rails disappearing into
tunnel of darkness;

where the two-seater thrill ride cars go
over not-swept-for-decades, concrete
passages;

where the satanic images are painted
on outdoor walls advertising what lies
within, skeletons and monsters;

All chipped and peeling now, unimposing
as long past billboard posts;

All the demons have retreated inside
to hide in their lairs, in their hideaways
behind floor and ceiling panels spring
triggered to open and leap at unexpected
angles, at unexpected times;

All colored lighted to emphasize
their glares, their deformed faces,
their threatening miens;

A sinister sound track added: maniacal,
fear gripped, primal in nature despite
Grade B, 40s movie budget of a dollar ninety-five

Timing and place are everything in a house
of horrors I rode in, hand gripping
my mother's as she, lost in a trance,
recited impressions of alternate lives
lived, places lurking inside this one,
images more fear inducing than any
cheap thrill induced effect.

Once inside the House of Horrors,
no one will hear you scream.

Woman Carrying a Child
Central Park, 1956

She could have been
my mother

With her almost shoulder
length dark hair

Angular facial lines

Not quite beautiful

Wearing that all-purpose-
camel hair overcoat
she wore in all kinds
of weather

She could be the same
woman who told me
it never got cold in
upstate NY

She should have known

She went to college there

And I believed her
more fool, I

Left for college and
a brutal winter where
temperatures routinely had
wind chills well below zero

That winter I contracted
double viral pneumonia

under dressed as I was
for frigid weather

In the photograph,
I could have been the small boy
asleep in the woman's arms

That woman with the worried,
preoccupied, downward
looking gaze

The kind of look my mother
always had when she went
places in her mind
no one was meant to go

She could have been
my mother if my actual
mother wasn't confined to
a nuthouse in 1956

I could have been loved

I could have been that child

Mother Cabrini, a disinterred saint in her glass and gold casket NYC, 1960

Exhumed in 1933 to facilitate
the process of becoming a saint.

Body parts removed and shipped
to various shrines.

Good works include: a sister of
Missionary of the Sacred Heart of Jesus
and Sacred Heart Orphan Asylum.

Beatified in 1938 for curing a
blind-in-one-eye child.

Canonized in 1946 for curing
a terminally ill congregate.

Is the patron saint of immigrants.

Was photographed, in state, by Diane Arbus
in 1960, presumably, after, the addition
of sculpted face mask and sculpted hands
to the holy body, for "a more life-like viewing"
experience.

Currently on permanent display in NYC
housed in a bronze casket with glass
for the faithful to better gaze upon her person.

All of this is normal, right?

Bishop of the Sea:
The Jersey Priestess in CA

End of days only come once in a lifetime
on California coastal cliffs, where the high
priestess of the apocalypse celebrates His
imminent arrival, by waving her Styrofoam
cross to better excite the winds the four horsemen
will be blown in with, as they ride on wave
crests, announcing His arrival.

At home, she worships in her: Our Lord Is Coming
nave, teary-eyed, staring at the hand-painted
image of long haired, fair skinned, Jesus
of yore, assured that while the end is near,
she will be among the number to be saved.

Replica rod and staff are leaning on a floral
papered wall by the four posted, canopy draped,
silk sheet bed, that is a safe haven for the faithful.

When asked what happens if the second coming
does not occur, or is delayed, she assures us
that scriptures will be consulted and a better
time arranged. "It has always been thus." She
says, smiling as she speaks.

James Dean in wax museum
Coney Island, 1957

Looks almost alive and
sweating like a contestant
in a rigged TV Quiz show,
like the $64,000 Dollar
Question, awaiting the final
clue, dramatic music added
to increase the tension,
watchers feel, but those inside,
not so much.

A small placard sized sign
says: James Dean Movie Star
Died 1954.

The unasked question remains:
Why was he speeding down
winding, blind curve mountain
highway, in top-down sports
car, so late into the night?

Unlike the quiz show question,
this one has no answer.

Mannequin in an Evening Gown
NYC, 1956

in sidewalk department store window
display is part Bette Davis, as ingénue
dressed for a bumpy ride, part embalmed
body, oddly displayed standing up,
behind a smeared with-finger-prints-
glass panels, a camera flash adding
a strange glow to stitched-closed-
for-the-funeral eyes. Only a nighthawk
could have seen the potential for this
shot, on nocturnal wanderings, up and down
city streets, seeing life frozen, in situ,
as no one had seen it before.

Imagine Diane Arbus as your wedding photographer.
Imagine if her creative vision had influenced her early work as a commercial artist.
Your cherished memories might look something like this:

A flower girl at a wedding
CT, 1964

Pity the poor flower girl dressed
for an outdoor, country club, wedding
and reception. Low fogs threatening
to envelop all the guests, her included,
holding, as she does, a basket for the
wedding party to be.

She is too young to know Melancholia,
though her face reveals a kind of innate
understanding well beyond her years.
Knows of a doomed celebration, end times,
solar winds, and worlds in collision
the bride, her sister and child, ride out
on a green, on the back nine, that abuts
the patio where the wedding party has
adjourned.

Is it fear or consternation, that makes
it impossible for her to smile?

Perhaps it is, the spirits of all those once-
living creatures that inhabited the white
fur wrap she wears, that have taken possession of her.

Trappers say the scream of dying
rabbits are uncanny, almost human.
It is the kind of sound no one but this
flower girl can hear.

The Madman from Massachusetts in an empty bar NYC, 1960

He could be anywhere alcohol is
served. Seeking shelter from the weather
to find worse storms within. Denied
service, he unleashes a vicious screed,
abusive words directed against the server.
The more he speaks, the less rooted to
reality his words are. Becomes a cataloging
of all the injustices he has endured during
a long life spent falling into an ever deepening,
ever widening, abyss that separates him
from the pay-their-own-way people.
He relates all those petty thefts,
cheating heart women, backstabbing
sneaky Pete sharers, on the beat, run-him-in
cops, social disservice workers, rejecting-
him-for-care psychiatric center personnel.
Projects a whole life of dismissal onto
the person behind the bar who has no more
time for his abuse.

Streeted, he seems more confused than ever.
Rubs the welt where his head hit the curb,
his torn-in-new-places pants and shirts
and the wounds beneath just beginning to bleed.
Upright, once again, he thrusts his palm out,
demanding loose change, or the folded bills
other folks carry, but there is no one there
to oblige him.

Clown in a Fedora
Palisades Park, NJ

After life, all textures will
be like these:

dark and grainy,
smoke choked

and crowded with
human shadows

waiting for a freak show

or ordering drinks
that will never come

Off duty, the unhappiest
clown ever, wears an
off-the-rack suit

and a hastily creased fedora

not so much sad faced
as disconsolate,
despairing,

as if suffering
from an unnamable dread,

the kind of angst
only a frozen soul
in an icehouse knows

Neither the grease paint
nor the expression on
his face can ever be removed

5 Members of Monster Fan Club
NYC, 1961

This group portrait is not some
American Gothic, that is, unless
you consider five six-year-old
kids, capable of a simulated a
grotesque.

Their masks seem to be a group effort
of pooled allowances taken to a Costumer
for rubber fright masks they are proudly
showing off as they sit as if on display,
side by side, on brownstone steps.

The temptation is to attribute something
to them that does not exist, given
that the portrait taker is Diane Arbus,
not someone like Winogrand or Frank.

Nor are they some kind of Ralph Meatyard
set piece like *A Romance for Ambrose Bierce,*
one of his Southern Gothic photos,
posed among old world ruins, of mansion remains,
left over from some Sherman march to the sea
with movie props, headless dolls, and
random limbs: hands, legs, arms, and collapsed covering-nothing,
masks. All posed beneath drooping cypress, moss-covered mounds,
in some Louisiana bayou nowhere.

No, these are kids in NYC, spontaneous Arbus quints not a
calculated surreality show,
But something suitable for a modern, illustrated Blake text
of Innocence and Experience.

Or am I seeing all of these photographs
wrong? Attributing innocence where
none exists? Who's to say?

Untitled #1

New meaning given
to the blind
leading the blind

in this case the barely
functional leading
the less functional

Part of a motley parade
on asylum grounds,
all the patients tricked out
for Halloween

Down's adults in
loose formation
following a determined
leader, who know where?

The leader, a woman,
holding the slowest
of slow learners

one of the terminally
confused with false moustache

ragged rude costume
permanently unfocused eyes

Is this the Great Escape?

Even if they made it
off the grounds

Where would they go?
What would they do?
Who would save them?

Untitled #2

If hell has a take-a-number
system where you will wait
in a common room
for an interview

that waiting area would
look like this:

an asylum morning room
with scuffed industrial
strength tile floor

molded plastic chairs
for the young men endlessly
rocking

for those gone-eyed humans
hugging themselves
as they compulsively sway,
moaning as they go

back and forth
back and forth

And chairs for the men
who balance them on
their feet as they lie
on the floor

maniacally laughing
even as the inevitable
chair fall
that splits swollen lips

And a chair for the woman
of no discernible age
wearing a pressed dress

standing guard over the little
red wagon

the kind of wagon kids use
to gather toys and dirt
and the refuse of life

So much depends on that
little red wagon
that signifies no more
than it actually is

Chances are,
where you are waiting,

that your number
will never be called

Untitled #3

They could be the wicker women,
elderly crones dressed in
mismatched clothes:

too small winter-weight jackets,
scarves and hats that cover their
thinning, unwashed hair,

plastic dime store masks
to hide who they really are.

They need no dress-up outfits,
no makeup to affect their look,
they are witch-like normally,

would have been burned or
drowned in an earlier age
instead of warehoused as they
are now.

They are five crones on the way
to an Autumn Rite where
the Wicker Man is waiting,

the one that has been built
on a common ground field between
asylum dorms,

built far enough away from human
habitation to prevent residual flames
from unintended ignitions once the offering
of the man has begun.

As they watch the flames,
their eyes contain memories
of rituals past:

of the festering heat,
cleansed flesh,
victuals flensed to
the bone.

None of them are allowed
the gift of fire.

Untitled #4

"This is not a dream.
  This is really happening."
          —Rosemary's Baby

Which movie was it?
Where Death was a man
with white grease painted face
able to be two places at once.

Lynch's Lost Highways.

Where a voice on the phone,
across town, a man is speaking to,
is Death, perhaps, and he is everywhere
and nowhere at once. Is also the man
with the glassine eyes and sinister smile,
standing next to our man as he listens
to the same person here and elsewhere.

This is one cocktail party
that man will never forget

Like the club date he played
his saxophone at, where the
white-faced man sits front row
in smoky venue and in the back
row as well.

No matter where he goes
Death is there before him
and after,

smiling as if he knows
something none of us
will never know,

like how we came to be
in this field with this
white faced person,

in a clean white sheet wearing
a death mask and posing
for a portrait holding a small
shopping bag for candy treats
instead of a scythe.

This is a picture that you
you can never unsee
once you have viewed it

every night
from now on

in the dark room
of your dreams.

Untitled #5

"We're not dreaming now."
—*Eyes Wide Shut*

So many of the costumed men
and women look as if they'd been
to the same costume rental Tom Cruise
used in *Eyes Wide Shut*

Where they rented a sheath dress or
a cape and cheap eye covering,
Lone Ranger masks

and went somewhere after the rental
they were never meant to be

Stood waiting on nearly frozen
asylum grounds or under suburban
Jersey sidewalk trees or on lawns
for a Satanic ritual to begin

All of them standing inert,
expectant, in the fading,
overcast daylight
for shadows to become night

They may be waiting still.

Untitled #6

They are the handmaidens of a witch's
coven, cast out of the fold and onto
the streets in their chiffon aprons and
street clothes, their made-in Arts & Crafts
wands, colored paper stars affixed to the end
of sticks, their party hats and out-for-the-day
shoes, two-bit plastic masks concealing
who they are from themselves.

They are wayfaring street creatures now,
standing on someone's front lawn for a
group portrait as human defects dressed to
do Halloween. All of them are smiling or
trying to, in-dusk-coming cooling down
afternoon in somewhere New Jersey.

They are arrested development super stars,
sentenced to childhood for life. Someone is
watching over them. There are so many worse
fates in life than this, as the portrait clearly shows.

Untitled # 7

Edward Curtis photographed
masks like these;
ceremonial ones
worn by native
American chiefs
warriors all

mythmaking,
photo shooting

There was mojo
in those masks, magic,
generational lore attached
to each one

worn with pride, earned pride

magic that gave the wearer
significant powers

Diane saw the power, the magic

the person inside the mask

the brown paper bag
with eye and nose
and mouth spaces cut out

saw the dime store string
hair the finger-painted designs

captured the power
the magic on a negative

held it for awhile
then let it go

Untitled #8

One of Weegee's special shots was
crowd reactions: facial expressions at
car crashes, murder scenes, the unloading
of paddy wagons . . . Those looks of horror,
the turning away, and the glancing back,
revulsion and awe, fear and excitement;
a kind of madness of crowds, this random
coming together brings before the Caucasian
white outline is drawn, the blood puddles,
sand covered then swept away . . .

Arbus would have known his work,
on the back pages of large circ. dailies,
a new horror for every working day and
weekends too.

Would have known how he was on call
24/7, had touts in bars, police stations,
taxi stands, ambulance driver staff rooms . . .

When you see the shot of the crowd of
women staring at an unseen, out-of-frame-
event. You can't help but be reminded of Weegee,
of fresh blood and open wounds, a horror show in
progress. But the viewer must wonder:
what horrific thing are they seeing? Is horror
relative? Given that these are a gaggle of adult,
Down's afflicted, gaping women, of all ages,
looking off stage at something that will forever
remain out of sight.
"What the hell are they looking at?"
What could be more unknowable that that?

Untitled #9

In the foreground of the picture,
a masked, dowdy older woman
of indeterminate age wears a
double breasted overcoat, clutches
a small bag, unaware of her
rolling down white socks bunching
over terminally scuffed shoes.
She looks at the portrait taker
through cut outs in a brown paper
shopping bag, holes too small for
seeing.

In the blurred background, an assembly
of fellow inmates at the asylum, are
gathering on a wide-open field that
could be one used for football if these
inmates could understand the rules
of a game more complicated than
Simon Says.

What are they doing back there?
So close together, running here
and there, while others stand as still
as the old woman in overcoat.
Maybe they are playing some kind
of supervised freeze tag game with
Death, one outlier has escaped from.
Or, maybe, she was simply, left behind
to stand as she stands now, for all time.

Untitled #10

What was it the Shakers sang?

'Tis the gift to be simple.

Applied here in the asylum
for women with mental handicaps,
where most of the people are smiling.
Seem unassuming, unself-conscious,
able to anticipate, to experience,
to enjoy dress-up day, an outing
on the town. Such joy is not easily
understood in people well past
childhood's end.

May seem incongruous, indecent even,
in a world where full faculty humans
are willful freaks.

Here's to all the ones born deformed,
too small, too tall, with too many limbs,
not enough, with genders all mixed up,
not one, or the other, or both.

Here's to all those others, who can only
have a normal life among others as messed up as they are.
Who live in sideshows,
curiosity cabinets, normal people look
inside in order to feel superior to another.

Here's to all those portraits of the women
of the asylum, in their dress-up clothes,
in their homemade costumes, their bathing
suits, paired with a special friend, holding
hands and feeling good.

Untitled #11 Revelations

Here's to the woman who shot a male
porno in progress then a wistful advert
for a *New York Times* special children's
fashion issue. Who took all those
dreamy, yearning shots of kids in a
semi-wild, idyllic place, breezes blowing
back the too tall grass, their no-longer
combed hair. Here's to the shooter who took
a picture for the cover, of a four-year-old
black boy and a four-year-old white girl
holding hands. In 1971. And how that picture was not used
on the cover. Was nowhere to be found in the issue
as if it were too horrible to be seen.

"The thing that's important to know is that
you never know. You're always sort of feeling your way."
—Diane Arbus, 1971

Still tied to the world
I cool off and lose
my form

Ozui, *Japanese Death Poem*

Selected List of Consulted Sources

Primary

Jeffrey Rosenheim, *Diane Arbus: in the beginning* Metropolitan Museum of Art distributed by Yale University Press 2016

Lee and Pultz, *Diane Arbus: Family Album,* Yale University Press 2003

Doon and Diane Arbus, *Diane Arbus*, Aperture Monograph 1972

Doon Arbus and Martin Israel: *Magazine Work*, Aperture 1984

Doon and Diane Arbus, *Diane Arbus: Untitled* Aperture 1995

Doon Arbus and Elizabeth Sussman, *Diane Arbus, Revelations,* Random House 2003

John Jacob and Diane Arbus, *A box of ten photographs*

Biographical

William Todd Schultz, *An Emergency in Slow Motion,* Bloomsbury USA, 2011

Arthur Lubow, *Diane Arbus: Portrait of a Photographer,* 2017

Patricia Bosworth, *Diane Arbus, A Biography,* Open Road Media 2012 reprint pb

Gregory Gibson, *Hubert's Freaks: The Rare Book-Dealer, The Times Square Talker and the Lost Photos of Diane Arbus,* Harcourt 2008

Magazine Articles

Stephen Frank, "Diane Arbus Revisited," B&W, Issue 36 April 2005

Tessa Decarlo, "A Fresh Look at Diane Arbus," Smithsonian 2004

Miscellaneous

Judith Keller, *Ralph Eugene Meatyard,* Phaidon Press 2002

Elizabeth Sussman, *Lisette Model,* Phaidon Press 2001

John von Hertz, *August Sander,* Aperture 1997

Mary Ellen Mark, *American Odyssey,* Aperture Monograph 2005

About the Author

Alan Catlin is retired from his unchosen profession as a barman. He has been publishing for parts of six decades in little, minuscule, not so little, literary, and university publications. Some of those would include the *Wormwood Review, The Wisconsin Review, Tray Full of Lab Rats*, *Wordsworth's Socks*, *The Literary Review,* and *Slipstream.*

His chapbook, *Blue Velvet*, won the Slipstream Chapbook Contest in 2017. One of his full-length books, *Last Man Standing* from Lummox Press, details his life and times walking to the bus stop, busing to work and to his former job. *Last Man Standing* is a continuation of *The Schenectady Chainsaw Massacre.* A transitional work, *Alien Nation* from March Street Press, combines four thematically-related chapbooks in one volume, paving the way from bar world, to social criticism, to his noir movie sequence, *Hollyweird.*

His latest volume of that work, *Exterminating Angels,* was published by Kelsay Books. A triptych *American Odyssey* includes three volumes of art related ekphrastic poems, two of which were published by Future Cycle Press and the third by Dos Madres. His ongoing current project is *Memories,* an epic in fragments that began during the Covid lockdown and continues to this day. Volume one was published by Alien Buddha as *Memories,* and volume two, as *Memories Too,* by Dos Madres. A collection of "real stories," reflections of a personal nature, *Listening to the Moonlight Sonata During a Mohs Procedure to Remove a Skin Cancer,* is scheduled for late 2023 by Impspired.

For his sins, he is the poetry and review editor of *misfitmagazine.net,* an online poetry journal.

www.ingramcontent.com/pod-product-compliance
Lightning Source LLC
LaVergne TN
LVHW020645100826
845148LV00012B/2343

* 9 7 8 1 6 3 9 8 0 3 8 7 3 *